This edition published in 2007 by

CHARTWELL BOOKS, INC.
A Division of
BOOK SALES, INC.
114 Northfield Avenue
Edison, New Jersey 08837

ISBN-13: 978-0-7858-2215-8
ISBN-10: 0-7858-2215-1

© 2007 Compendium Publishing, 43 Frith Street, London, Soho, W1V 4SA, United Kingdom

Cataloging-in-Publication data is available from the Library of Congress

Printed and bound in China

Design: Ian Hughes/Compendium Design

Page 2: Fisherman's Wharf is San Francisco's most popular tourist destination and boasts many seafood restaurants, street vendors, and souvenir stores as well as continuing to operate as a fishing wharf.

Pages 3-4: The skyline of San Francisco's Financial District dominated by the city's two tallest skyscrapers, the Bank of America Building and the Transamerica Pyramid.

SAN FRANCISCO

THE GROWTH OF THE CITY

CHARTWELL
BOOKS, INC.

SAN FRANCISCO

THE GROWTH OF THE CITY

CHARTWELL
BOOKS, INC.

This edition published in 2007 by

CHARTWELL BOOKS, INC.
A Division of
BOOK SALES, INC.
114 Northfield Avenue
Edison, New Jersey 08837

ISBN-13: 978-0-7858-2215-8
ISBN-10: 0-7858-2215-1

© 2007 Compendium Publishing, 43 Frith Street, London,
Soho, W1V 4SA, United Kingdom

Cataloging-in-Publication data is available from the Library
of Congress

Printed and bound in China

Design: Ian Hughes/Compendium Design

Page 2: Fisherman's Wharf is San Francisco's most popular tourist
destination and boasts many seafood restaurants, street vendors, and
souvenir stores as well as continuing to operate as a fishing wharf.

Pages 3-4: The skyline of San Francisco's Financial District
dominated by the city's two tallest skyscrapers, the Bank of America
Building and the Transamerica Pyramid.

Contents

Introduction

An aerial view of the skyscrapers that form the skyline of the Financial District at the heart of modern-day San Francisco.

Introduction

Situated on the tip of a peninsular overlooking the mouth of the vast San Francisco Bay on the West Coast of North America, the city of San Francisco is renowned as one of the most visually stunning in the world. It is the fourth largest city in California and the fourteenth largest in the United States. With a population of around 750,000 occupying an area of forty-seven square miles, it is second only to New York in terms of population density. Famous for the fog that frequently enshrouds the city, steep winding hills, and internationally recognized landmarks such as the Golden Gate Bridge and Alcatraz Island, San Francisco is also renowned for its liberal, left-wing counter-culture embodied in the Beat scene of the 1950s, the "Turn On, Tune In, Drop Out" Flower Power era of the Haight-Ashbury district in the 1960s, and in more recent times by the flourishing gay community that makes up an estimated fifteen per cent of the city's population.

Compared to many areas of the United States, San Francisco remained undiscovered by Europeans for a long time. Several early explorers, including the English privateer Sir Francis Drake in 1579, sailed past the San Francisco Peninsular without even noticing the huge bay that lay inside the mouth of the Golden Gate. This failure is most likely explained by the thick fogs that are still familiar to San Franciscans today. In fact, it wasn't until 1769 that the Spaniard Jose Francisco Ortega found the entrance to San Francisco Bay. Seven years later, in 1776 (the same year that the nascent United States of America was making its Declaration of Independence) the first party of Spanish colonists arrived in the area and built the Mission San Francisco de Asís (which would later become known as the Mission Dolores) and its attendant *presidio* (fort).

For the remainder of the eighteenth century and in the first two decades of the nineteenth century, the Spanish carried out a similar pattern of colonization across California, establishing a total of twenty-one missions. From 1770 onward, Russian settlers, trappers, and fur-traders joined the Spanish in California: the memory of these San Franciscan pioneers lives on in the name of the Russian Hill district. The city is also still currently home to a sizeable Russian community.

In 1821, following the Mexican War of Independence, California gained its independence from Spain and became, for a brief time, part of the Mexican Republic. It was during this period, in 1835 to be exact, that the town of Yerba Buena, which would go on to become San Francisco, was founded. Although the tiny town was blessed by good anchorage on the bay, it lacked a natural water supply, and growth was limited over the following decade. By 1845, just over 100 people resided in Yerba Buena, occupying little more than twenty buildings.

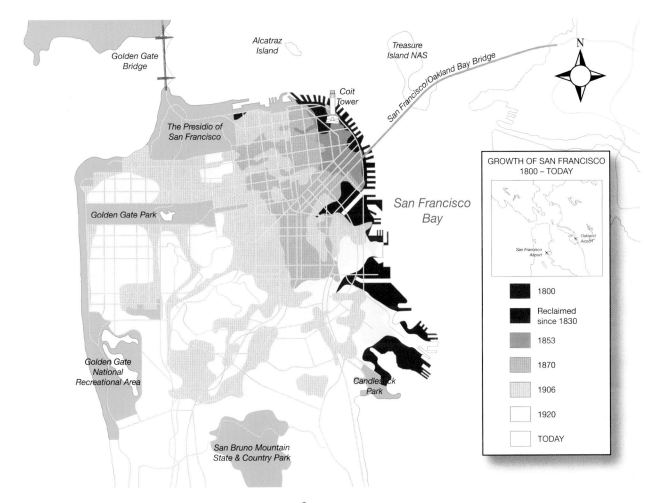

Golden Gate
Bridge

Alcatraz
Island

Treasure
Island NAS

San Francisco/Oakland Bay Bridge

N

Coit
Tower

The Presidio of
San Francisco

Golden Gate Park

San Francisco
Bay

Golden Gate
National
Recreational Area

Candlestick
Park

San Bruno Mountain
State & Country Park

GROWTH OF SAN FRANCISCO
1800 – TODAY

Oakland
Airport

San Francisco
Airport

1800

Reclaimed
since 1830

1853

1870

1906

1920

TODAY

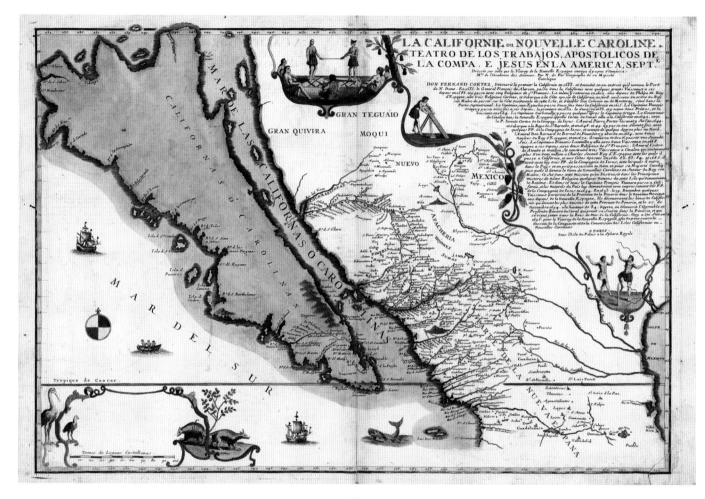

In 1846, during the Mexican-American War, Yerba Buena, along with the rest of California was claimed by the United States. In 1847, the town was renamed San Francisco by *alcalde* (mayor) Washington Bartlett and the following year, under the terms of the Treaty of Guadalupe, San Francisco and the rest of California was formally ceded to the United States. By this time, San Francisco boasted seventy-nine buildings and streets that are still in use today, albeit renamed: today's Pacific Street was then known as Bartlett Street, while a stretch of Sacramento Street was also in existence, as Howard Street.

The discovery of gold at Sutter's Mill in the Sierra Nevada foothills in the January of 1848 signaled a massive surge in growth for the newly American town. By the end of that year, news of the find had spread across the United States and gold fever swept the nation. Hordes of prospectors (known as '49ers) began to arrive in San Francisco on their way to the hills in search of gold. It is

LEFT: A map of the West Coast of America dating to the early 1700s. For many years European explorers mistakenly believed that California was an island.

BELOW: An 1812 illustration showing a group of native Miwok Indians canoeing across San Francisco Bay. The buildings of the Mission Dolores and the *presidio* can be seen nestled at the foot of the hills.

estimated that in 1849 alone over 100,000 people passed through the town and by the end of that year the population had risen dramatically from a few hundred to well over 20,000. At this time there were still relatively few permanent buildings in San Francisco. The city was mostly constructed of tents and shacks, quickly erected to cope with the sudden influx of people. Over the next few years, however, more solid structures such as schools, churches, and theaters were built as gold began to pour in to San Francisco. Pacific Heights and Noe Valley were also annexed to provide room for the city to spread. The newfound wealth on offer in the burgeoning town attracted all manner of characters and San Francisco soon became a wild, frontier town where gambling, prostitution, and violence were rife. Not all was lawlessness though; San Francisco's Financial District was also born in the Gold Rush years. By 1854, however, the supply of gold had dwindled and the rush drew to a close. The streets now began to fill with ex-miners who suddenly had few prospects. Businesses that had thrived in the boom years struggled to stay afloat.

The depression that followed the end of the Gold Rush was to prove short: the 1860s saw more mineral mining, this time of the Comstock silver lode on the slopes of Mount Davidson in western Nevada and the building of the Central Pacific Railroad, events that made multi-millionaires of some San Franciscans and

provided a more sustained period of growth and prosperity for the city. The Comstock Lode, which was the largest deposit of silver ore ever discovered in the U.S., generated fabulous wealth, but the three men who made the original discovery—Peter O'Riley, Patrick McLaughlin and Henry Comstock—all died in poverty. Nevertheless, entrepreneurs such as James Flood made their fortunes investing in the silver mines and as their wealth began to flow into San Francisco, lavish homes and ornate civic buildings began to line the streets that had not so long ago been home to nothing more than tents and shacks. By the time the lode was exhausted and the mines abandoned in 1898, 400 million dollars had been generated. The year 1860 also saw the city's first horse-drawn street car service begin.

The Central Pacific Railroad was the western half of the First Transcontinental Railroad that linked the east and west coasts of the U.S. Work began in 1863 and was completed, with the ceremonial hammering of a golden spike, on May 10 1869. The completion of the rail link reduced journeys that had previously taken up to eight months by land or sea to a matter of days. Imported Chinese laborers, known as "coolies," carried out the majority of the construction work, but those who benefited most from the building of the railroad were its backers, the "Big Four" of Leland Stanford, Collis Huntington, Charles Crocker, and Mark Hopkins, all of whom built luxurious houses at the top of Nob Hill. These four men made vast fortunes and garnered huge political influence. The sharp business practices that they employed led to them being popularly known as the "Robber Barons." By the

LEFT: An 1871 picture entitled "Gold Mining In California" by Currier & Ives. The discovery of gold transformed San Francisco from a sleepy backwater into a thriving city.

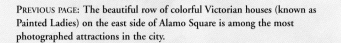

PREVIOUS PAGE: The beautiful row of colorful Victorian houses (known as Painted Ladies) on the east side of Alamo Square is among the most photographed attractions in the city.

BELOW: A view of Union Square in 1910. The square takes its name from the pro-Union rallies that were held here during the Civil War. In the center can be seen the recently erected *Victory* monument celebrating Admiral Dewey's victory over the Spanish Navy at Manila Bay in the Philippines, on May 1, 1898 during the Spanish-American War.

1870s, the Chinese made up around twenty per cent of San Francisco's population, a statistic that still holds. Indeed, the Chinatown district in San Francisco is one of the largest in the nation. However, once work on the railroads had dried up the Chinese faced terrible discrimination and the threat of violence was never far away.

During the 1870s, San Francisco also began spreading into the suburbs. The introduction of cable cars meant that the steep hills could now be easily traveled for the first time, and downtown workers began to build homes along the lines.

By the end of the nineteenth century, San Francisco's population had risen to over 300,000. It was now the most affluent city in California and the largest in the U.S. west of Chicago. However, in 1906 the city was to be struck by disaster. On April 18 of that year, an earthquake struck the city. Although it lasted less than a minute, the quake and the fires that followed destroyed the city almost entirely. In fact, 3,000 people were killed and a quarter of a million lost their homes. Nevertheless, San Francisco was able to make a swift recovery—thanks in large part to the eight million dollars of aid that arrived from around the world in the weeks following the disaster—and the city was rebuilt astonishingly quickly. So impressive was the resurgence of the city that by 1915 San Francisco was playing host to the Panama-Pacific Exposition, a lavish world's fair. In 1918, San Francisco opened the world's longest subway tunnel. The Twin Peaks Tunnel encouraged building west of the peaks, resulting in the new neighborhoods of Forest Hill, West Portal, St. Francis Wood, and Westwood Park.

RIGHT: An aerial view of Fort Mason. During World War II the fort was a major facility for the U.S. forces with over 1.5 million servicemen embarking for the conflict from its wharves. It also served in a similar capacity during the Korean War of the 1950s.

In this view from the Marin
Headlands, the twin towers of the
Golden Gate Bridge, completed in
1937, jut above the dense fog that is
as much a feature of San Francisco as
the bridge itself.

The following decades were comparatively lucky ones for the city. While the First World War tore Europe apart it had little impact on San Francisco, beyond providing a brief boost for the city's manufacturing industries. The Depression that crippled large swathes of America during the 1930s also had less of an effect on San Francisco than on many U.S. cities, though some building work ground to a halt during these years. The O'Shaughnessy Seawall, which was intended to extend Ocean Beach, was stopped at Lincoln Avenue while the city's skyline remained static through to the fifties. Notable exceptions, however, include sites that are now synonymous with the modern city; Coit Tower was completed in 1933 and the Golden Gate Bridge in 1937.

World War II was to have a far greater influence on San Francisco as workers poured into the city to man the shipyards at Sausalito and Richmond as well as the port and factories that went into overdrive to service the war effort. Many of the servicemen who returned from the conflict stayed on in the city and made their homes there.

Through the latter part of the twentieth century and the beginning of the twenty-first, San Francisco witnessed great changes and momentous events. In 1945 the first headquarters of the United Nations was established in the city. The war with Japan was also formally ended with the signing of a peace treaty by the Japanese premier at the War Memorial Opera House in 1951. While skyscrapers raised the skyline during the late 1960s, the city was at the forefront of the counter-culture that embodied that decade. Throughout the "Summer of Love" in 1967 thousands of young people flocked to the Haight-Ashbury district that was at the heart of the emerging hippie scene. Local bands such as the Grateful Dead and Jefferson Airplane became household names across the world and the "Human Be-In" was held in Golden Gate Park. In 1972, the first Gay Pride parade was held in the Castro District and in 1974 Harvey Milk became the first openly gay person to be elected to city's Board of Supervisors. Following the assassination of Milk and Mayor George Moscone by Dan White in 1978, Dianne Feinstein began a ten-year tenure as mayor with huge backing from the gay community of San Francisco. Feinstein went on to be elected to the U.S. Senate in 1992.

On October 17, 1989, the Loma Prieta Earthquake hit San Francisco. The loss of life was far less than in the quake of 1906, partly because it struck just before game three of the 1989 World Series featuring two of the Bay Area's local teams and the majority of San Franciscans were either at the game or indoors watching it on television. The disaster gave San Franciscans the opportunity to re-evaluate their city. The demolition of the quake-damaged Embarcadero Freeway allowed the city to open up and renew the historic waterfront area. Encouraged by the beautification of the waterfront, the final years of the twentieth century saw a host of other renovation works, notably in the South of Market (SOMA) district and at the Ferry Building. Although the city has since been hit hard by the bursting of the dot-com bubble, San Francisco has, as ever, fought to recover from adversity and remains a vibrant, creative, and beautiful city that is renowned and admired around the world.

Situated in the grounds of the Presidio and opened in 2005, the Letterman Digital Arts Center is the new home for George Lucas's phenomenally successful Lucasfilm Ltd. special effects studio. The siting of the facility in San Francisco reflects both the regeneration of the city in the wake of the dot-com collapse and its long-held reputation for fostering the creative arts.

From Colony Years to Gold Rush: 1769–1860

An 1851 view of San Francisco, two years after the Gold Rush had begun. The harbor is teeming with ships; prospectors hoping to make their fortunes are still arriving and pitching their tents in the area around town.

From Colony Years to Gold Rush: 1769–1860

Under Spanish rule the area that is modern-day San Francisco consisted of little more than the religious mission (the Mission Dolores) and a fort (*presidio*) to guard it. Overlooked by European sailors for so long, once discovered Spain showed little inclination to expand its interests there. Ironically, while efforts to colonize the New World were largely driven by the search for treasure and wealth, less than thirty years after the Spanish ceded control of California it was to prove to have gold in abundance.

Following independence from Spain in 1821 growth remained slow. The first significant house in Yerba Buena (as San Francisco was then called) was built by the Englishman William Richardson in 1835 when he was appointed harbor master. A year later the pioneer Jacob Leese arrived and set up a mercantile business. Despite these momentous events in the tiny community, the little town remained as overlooked for decades as the bay itself had once been.

California became part of the United States in 1848, following the Mexican War, but it was the Gold Rush of 1849 that was to prove the spur for serious growth. In the two years following the discovery of gold in California, the population of San Francisco exploded and in 1850 it was incorporated as a city. Soon after, it was stretching its wings in a series of annexations. As people began to arrive in droves, homes and businesses were thrown up as quickly as they could be. By necessity these were almost all temporary wooden and canvas structures and between 1849 and 1851 the town was ravaged by fire no less than six times, often in suspicious circumstance, which soon led to legislation that required all new buildings to be of brick or stone construction.

Despite this, San Francisco was undoubtedly thriving as the commercial and transportation hub of the Gold Rush region. And though the supply of gold had dried up by 1854, by 1859 it became apparent that the hills further inland had far more wealth to offer when the Comstock Lode was discovered in 1859.

RIGHT: A drawing of the recently renamed town of San Francisco in 1847, showing U.S. navy ships in the harbor of the very small town. It was in this year that Yerba Beuna became the Town of San Francisco under mayor Washington Bartlett.

Mission Dolores

The oldest building still standing in San Francisco, the Mission Dolores was constructed between 1782 and 1791. One of the numerous missions that were established by the Spanish Franciscans in California, the first Mission San Francisco de Asís, as it was originally known, was a simple wooden structure that was dedicated in 1776.

Over time the mission became known as the Mission Dolores due to the close vicinity of the now vanished Lago de los Dolores (Lake of Our Lady of Sorrows). Although the current mission has been changed in many ways over the intervening years, the facade of the Mission chapel that can be seen today is much the same as when it was first built.

LEFT: By 1880, when this photograph was taken, the mission was the last remnant of the earlier, quieter days before the Gold Rush of 1849 turned San Francisco from a sleepy village into a bustling metropolis.

RIGHT: A modern view of the restored facade of the Mission Dolores. To the right can be seen the towers of the rebuilt basilica (the original having been destroyed by the 1906 earthquake).

LEFT: The cemetery in the grounds is one of the very few graveyards that remain within the city limits. To the left can be seen a statue of the Father Junípero Serra who was a pivotal figure in the establishment of Franciscan missions throughout California during Spanish occupation.

RIGHT: The gravestone of Luis Antonio Argüello, the first governor of Alta California, from 1822–25. During the period of Mexican rule, Argüello was the first native Californian to serve in this office. Prior to holding this post, in 1821, he had made the most wide-ranging exploration of the area attempted by the Spanish.

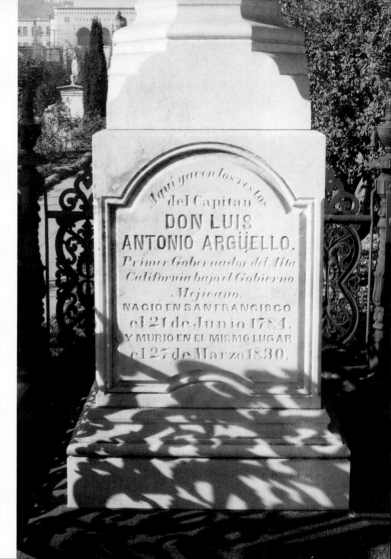

On the ceiling, over the nave of the Mission Dolores, can be seen painted redwood beams that were originally crafted by Native-American workers. At the far end of the nave is the ornate altarpiece, which was installed in 1796.

ABOVE: This view shows the harbor just two years after the picture on page 27. In 1849, at the start of the Gold Rush, the bay is far more crowded and the town is beginning to expand dramatically.

RIGHT: Day Ju, one of the first Chinese to arrive in San Francisco, founded the original Tin How Temple in 1852. It can now be found on the top floor of 125 Waverly Place and is the oldest Chinese temple still in use in the U.S.

LEFT: Parrot's Granite Block, seen here, was built during the 1850s using pre-cut granite blocks that were imported from China. The first recorded strike by Chinese workers striving for equal pay occurred during its construction.

RIGHT: Situated at the tip of the San Francisco Peninsular (these days in the shadow of the Golden Gate Bridge), Fort Point was built by the U.S. Army between 1853 and 1861 with the dual purpose of defending San Francisco Bay and protecting ships transporting gold from the mines inland.

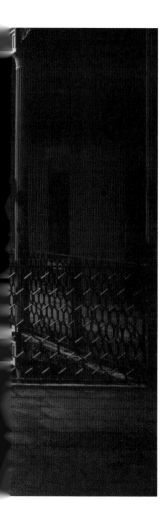

LEFT: An interior view of the courtyard of Fort Point. Despite its prominent position and the wealth it guarded, the fort never saw action and was retired from military service in 1900. The building is now open to the public.

RIGHT: The Wells Fargo building on Montgomery Street was the first brick building to be erected in San Francisco. Wells Fargo and Co. was founded in 1852 and went on to become one of the most prominent and influential companies in the West. A Wells Fargo History Museum can be found at 420 Montgomery Street.

LEFT: Dedicated in 1854, Old St. Mary's Cathedral was the first Catholic Cathedral in San Francisco. The inscription below the clock reads "Son, observe the time and fly from evil" and is believed to refer to the brothels that lined the street opposite the church at the time of its construction.

BELOW: This attractive, hand-colored lithograph from 1860 shows the streets and houses of the rapidly expanding San Francisco. Residents of the city enjoy a stroll on the hills overlooking the bay.

Alcatraz

Sitting in the middle of San Francisco Bay, for many years Alcatraz Island was the most famous prison in the world, known to millions as "The Rock." This barren island, surrounded by dangerous currents, was first named "La Isla de los Alcatraces" (Island of the Pelicans) by the Spanish explorer Juan Manuel de Ayala in 1775. It remained largely untouched until the early 1850s when its strategic location led the U.S. Army to begin the construction of a military fortress. The island's isolated location also made it an ideal location for a prison and it first began to serve in this function during the Civil War. By the end of the Spanish-American War in 1898 the inmate population had risen to almost 500.

In 1934 the military ceased to use the facility and Alcatraz became a federal penitentiary that went on to house such famous inmates as Al Capone, Machine Gun Kelly, and Robert Stroud (the "Birdman of Alcatraz"). It was during this incarnation that Alcatraz gained its reputation for having an extremely harsh prison regime.

On March 21, 1963 Alcatraz was closed as a prison facility. The island remained unoccupied until 1969 when it was taken over by a group of American Indians who were campaigning to have Alcatraz recognized as Indian land. The occupation lasted for eighteen months and led to the destruction of several buildings including the warden's house. The Indians did however manage to win many concessions from the U.S. government as a direct result of their actions.

Alcatraz Island is now open to the public and since 1972 has been part of the Golden Gate National Recreation Area.

RIGHT: This photograph shows the ruins of the Officers' Club, a building that dates from the time of Alcatraz's use as a military fort. It was used as a recreational facility during the island's time as a federal penitentiary.

BELOW: A view of the north end of the island, showing the industries building, water tower, power plant, and the recreation yard (in the left foreground). Prisoners were passed through a metal detector as they moved to and from the exercise yard.

RIGHT: The cell house as seen from the exercise yard. The "Big House," as it was known to inmates, housed four separate cell blocks. The building was constructed on the foundations of the original military fortress.

LEFT: A group of Sioux Indians seen demonstrating at Alcatraz to draw attention to their claim that the island should be recognized as Indian land under the terms of a nineteenth century treaty with the U.S. government.

RIGHT: Alcatraz's cells were designed so that none of them had either an outside wall or ceiling. Today, they are one of San Francisco's most popular tourist destinations.

"The Rock" as seen from San
Francisco Bay. The cell house that
held the prisoners is the large
building at the top left of the island.

NEVADA BLOCK.

CALVARY CHURCH.

SANSOME STREET.

PALACE HOTEL.

RUSS HOUSE MONTGOMERY STREET.

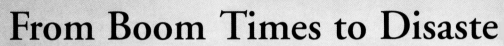

From Boom Times to Disaste

MURPHY, GRANT & CO'S BUILDING SANSOME STREET.

ORIENTAL BLOCK.

SA

CALIFORNIA STREET, CORNER SANSOME.

MERCANTILE LIBRARY BUSH STREET.

MONTGOMERY STREET.

P.M.S.S. CO'S

GRAND HOTEL

LONDON & S FR BANK

S. MARYS CATHEDRAL

CLIFF HOUSE

861–1906

A panorama of San Francisco surrounded by twenty-two views of buildings and street scenes in San Francisco, published in 1874 by Frederick Hess.

LICK HOUSE

ISCO

THE WHITE HOUSE.

NA AND JAPAN

CALIFORNIA STREET

OCCIDENTAL HOTEL

CORNER FIRST AND MARKET STREET.

CORNER GEARY AND KEARNY STREET.

From Boom Times to Disaster: 1861–1906

The discovery of the Comstock silver lode signaled the start of lasting boom times for San Francisco. Fortunes were made and lost at the San Francisco Stock Exchange, which was opened in 1862, with over 2,000 mining companies registered at the height of trading. Nevertheless, parts of San Francisco remained rowdy and untamed despite the efforts of the Committees of Vigilance during the previous decade. In the 1860s, the infamous Barbary Coast district, centred on modern-day Jackson Square, teemed with opium dens, brothels, saloons, and gambling houses where the unwary were soon parted from their money.

Like many cities across the United States, the development of this unique city—part rowdy frontier town, part affluent metropolis— was further enhanced by the arrival of the railroad. The building of the Central Pacific Railroad, completed in 1869, dramatically reduced travel times between the east and west coasts of America and made its backers fabulously wealthy. But these were also to be times of contrasting fortunes for San Francisco's population. When work became scarce, the Chinese, who had begun to arrive during the Gold Rush and who had labored on the railroads, became the focus of the mob mentality that had earlier led to forming of the Committees of Vigilance. In 1877, there was a running riot between the whites and Chinese that lasted for two days and in 1882 Congress passed the Chinese Exclusion Act, banning further Chinese immigration. The act was not repealed until 1943.

Throughout these troubled times the city itself continued to grow and prosper. In 1870, plans were drawn up for a vast public recreational area that would become Golden Gate Park and in 1873 the world's first street cable cars, invented by Andrew S. Hallidie, began operating in San Francisco. As the nineteenth century drew to a close the majority of San Franciscans had every right to be optimistic about the future. Tragically, disaster was just around the corner. In 1906 the largest earthquake to ever hit the city devastated San Francisco.

RIGHT: The unusual looking Octagon House at 2645 Gough Street was built in 1861. It currently houses a small museum displaying a collection of artwork and documentation from the nineteenth century.

LEFT: Although it was destroyed by fire during the 1906 earthquake, the Lick House was, at the time of its construction in the 1860s, one of the most luxurious hotels in the West. The hotel was situated at the intersection of Montgomery Street and Sutter Street and contained a dining room that could seat 400.

RIGHT: Solomon Gump, a German-Jewish immigrant, founded Gump's department store in 1861. The store that can still be found at 135 Post Street is famous for its lavish window displays.

Golden Gate Park

Stretching from Haight-Ashbury on its eastern border to the Pacific Ocean on the west, Golden Gate Park measures eight blocks wide by fifty-two blocks long and covers 1,040 acres. As the city prospered during the 1860s, San Francisco's citizens began to clamour for a large public park to match Central Park that was under construction in New York. The city authorities put the planning and construction of the proposed park in the hands of the field engineer William Hammond Hall, who prepared a plan in 1870 and was appointed as its superintendent in 1871.

The land on which the park was to be built, known at the time as the "Outside Lands," was not the most obvious site for a lush, green public park. In fact, the area was a virtual wasteland of sand dunes, but Hall overcame this problem by planting deep-rooted sea grass and yellow lupine to convert the area into a verdant park. In the late 1800s, Hall appointed John McLaren, who would later succeed him as the park's superintendent, as his assistant. The pair's shared vision for the park was that it should be natural environment and Hall was particularly opposed to the holding of the 1894 California Midwinter Fair in the park, though it went ahead despite his objections. Today, though Golden Gate Park holds far more buildings than Hall had originally planned, his vision of a public park that would provide a welcome break from urban life is still enjoyed by San Franciscans.

RIGHT: A modern, aerial view of Golden Gate Park (with the shore of the Pacific Ocean in the foreground) surrounded by the urban sprawl that it was designed to offer an escape from.

The Conservatory of Flowers opened in 1879 and is the oldest extant building in the park. It was severely damaged during a storm in 1995, but following a public campaign it was fully restored and reopened in 2003.

LEFT: One of the most popular attractions in the park is the Japanese Tea Garden that was originally built as part of the 1984 California Midwinter Fair.

RIGHT: Music lovers in 1902 enjoying a concert at the Spreckels Temple of Music. The building has been the site of free concerts every Sunday since 1899.

LEFT: Originally built in 1903 to pump water as part of the park's irrigation system, the Dutch Windmill is now purely ornamental. It is located in the Queen Wilhelmina Tulip Garden in the northwest of the park.

RIGHT: The state-of-the-art de Young Museum was opened in 2005 following the destruction of the original building in the 1989 earthquake. Since its inception in 1895 the museum has been home to one of San Francisco's most fabulous collections of fine art.

LEFT: One of the many theaters and opera houses that sprang up as wealth flooded into the city was the Metropolitan on Montgomery Street. This building was also lost to fire in 1906.

RIGHT: This building was the headquarters of the San Francisco & San Jose Railroad Company that began offering travel along the Peninsula corridor on October 18, 1863.

Seen here in an 1873 photograph is the Chapel of Our Lady in the grounds of the Presidio. Built in 1864, the chapel and its grounds occupy the site of the original Spanish fort built in 1776.

The lighthouse on Yerba Buena Island, in the middle of San Francisco Bay, was built in 1875 and remains operational to this day. Since 1958 it has been automated and the former lighthouse keeper's home is now the residence of a Coast Guard admiral. The island itself had its name changed officially in 1895 to Goat Island, but in 1931 this decision was reversed and it returned to its former name.

Cable Cars

The first cable car line in San Francisco was opened to the public on September 1, 1873, and run by the Clay Street Hill Railroad. Its inventor, Andrew Smith Hallidie, had been inspired by the sight of a bad accident involving a horse that collapsed as it struggled to heave a tram up the slippery slopes of Jackson Street. Such was the success of the Clay Street Hill Railroad that by the time of the 1906 earthquake there were eight companies running cable car lines in the city, utilizing over 600 cars across a network of fifty-three miles of track.

Following the earthquake and partly due to the advent of the cheaper electric streetcar, only some of the cable car lines were rebuilt. By 1947, buses had also become a cheaper alternative to the cable cars and Mayor Roger Lapham proposed that the lines should be closed for good. This prompted Friedel Klussmann to start a public campaign to save the cable cars. Eventually a referendum was held on the subject and an overwhelming majority voted to keep the cable cars. Since then the entire remaining network has been rebuilt and the system, the last of its kind in the world, has become synonymous with the city of San Francisco.

RIGHT: A photograph showing Andrew S. Hallidie (on the left) at the controls of the first Clay Street Hill Railroad cable car on September 1, 1873.

#1117 Washington & Mason Power House 12-21-06

LEFT: A December 1906 photograph that shows the start of reconstruction work on the powerhouse and car barn following its destruction in the earthquake of that year.

RIGHT: The Cable Car Barn now serves as both the powerhouse of the cable car system and as a museum of the history of the cable cars in San Francisco.

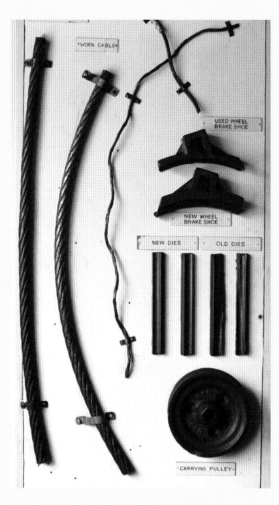

LEFT: Cables, brake wheels, and other cable car parts on display in the Cable Car Barn Museum at 1201 Mason Street.

RIGHT: A cable car operator turns a car on a roundabout. A highly skilled driver, known as the grip man, and a conductor who collects fares and organizes the barding and alighting of passengers, man each cable car.

A cable car running along Nob Hill. The cars are now designated historic monuments and great care is taken to preserve historical authenticity.

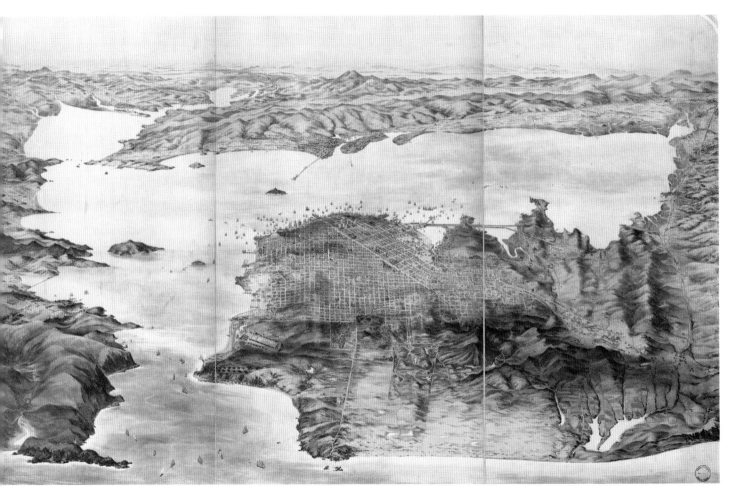

Two birds eye views of San Francisco; the first (LEFT) drawn by G. H. Goddard in 1876 is a view from the Pacific Ocean overlooking San Francisco and surrounding countryside. The second (ABOVE) drawn by C. R. Parsons in 1878 is a view from the bay looking southwest. Both maps show San Francisco as a thriving city with a bustling port full of ships.

LEFT: This impressive mansion was built in 1885 for William Flood and was one of the few buildings on Nob Hill to survive the fires in 1906. After the earthquake, the Pacific-Union Club bought the residence and it houses the club to this day.

RIGHT: The Gothic-looking Haas-Lilienthal House at 2007 Franklin Street was built in 1886 for the wealthy merchant William Haas. In 1972 the house was given to the San Francisco Architectural Heritage and it now houses a museum replete with furniture and furnishings that allow the visitor to experience the sumptuous lifestyle enjoyed by the well-to-do citizens of late nineteenth century San Francisco.

LEFT AND RIGHT: A. Page Brown designed the Ferry Building in 1892. The 230 foot clock tower was inspired by La Giralda, the bell tower of Seville Cathedral. In its heyday during the early 1930s, 170 ferries a day departed from the Ferry Building. However, the building of the Bay and Golden Gate bridges in 1936 and 1937 doomed the ferry services. It was re-opened in 2003 following a seventy-five million dollar restoration and now houses a thriving marketplace.

Left: The Polk-Williams House is in fact two houses under one roof. The architect Willis Polk designed the building in 1892 for the painter Mrs. Virgil Williams and waived his fee in return for roughly one third of the lot. The white door numbered 1017 was the entrance to the Polk home. Under the apex of the outbuilding on the right of the picture the number 1019 can just be made out; this was the address of the Williams home.

RIGHT: Willis Polk designed the Merchant's Building at 465 California Street in 1903. The interior of the building is decorated with nautical themed paintings by William Coulter while the lookout tower (below the flagpole) allowed observers to watch for the safe return of merchant ships.

THE MERCHANTS' EXCHANGE, SAN FRANCISCO, CALIFORNIA,

LEFT: Two turreted, Queen Anne-style houses in Alamo Square. These beautiful, ornate Victorian era homes were built for wealthy San Franciscans in the 1890s.

RIGHT: The Westin St. Francis Hotel at 335 Powell Street has been a feature of Union Square since it was built in 1904. The thirty-two-storey block behind the three original towers of the hotel was added in the 1970s.

1906 Earthquake

At around 05.00am on April 18, 1906, an earthquake more powerful than any other to hit the city struck San Francisco. Caused by a 270 mile rupture of the San Andreas Fault, the quake has since been estimated as measuring 7.8 on the Richter scale. The effects on the city were devastating: hundreds of buildings collapsed, water mains throughout the city burst and fires burned for days before they could be bought under control. Around eighty percent of the city was destroyed and the death toll came to over 3,000 (though at the time, in an effort to assuage public morale, it was announced officially as being in the hundreds rather than thousands). Around a quarter of a million people were made homeless. Despite the devastation, San Francisco recovered incredibly quickly and by 1910 the majority of the city had been rebuilt.

RIGHT: A view from the St. Francis Hotel, taken on April 18, the day the earthquake struck, this photograph shows clouds billowing over San Francisco as the city burns.

THE BURNING OF SAN FRANCISCO APRIL 18. COPYRIGHT 1906.

The luxurious mansions of the "Robber Barons," Leland Stanford, Mark Hopkins, Charles Crocker, and Collis P. Huntington on Nob Hill were all primarily constructed of wood and as such were completely destroyed by the fire. This view from the top of Nob Hill, overlooking the city, shows the ruins of these once magnificent homes.

A panoramic view of the Western Addition and the Mission, showing the ruins of City Hall and St. Ignatius College, with Twin Peaks and Strawberry Hill in the distance.

Three photographs taken in the wake of the earthquake that portray the effects of the destruction. The first (New Image) shows frame houses tumbled from their foundation, while the photograph (New Image 2) shows San Franciscans venturing out along California Street. The Merchants Exchange is to the left. The final photograph (3C25749) shows a family picking among the rubble of their house in search of lost family treasures.

This photograph shows a view from the street of the tent city in Jefferson Square. Following the quake, over 100,000 people spent the summer of 1906 living in refugee camps such as this.

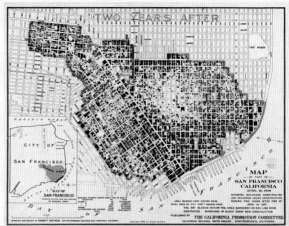

ABOVE: A map issued by the California Promotion Committee in 1908 showing buildings constructed and buildings under construction during the two years following the earthquake and fire.

LEFT: A panoramic view of the ruins of the city taken from the Lawrence Captive Airship, 2,000 feet above San Francisco Bay overlooking the waterfront.

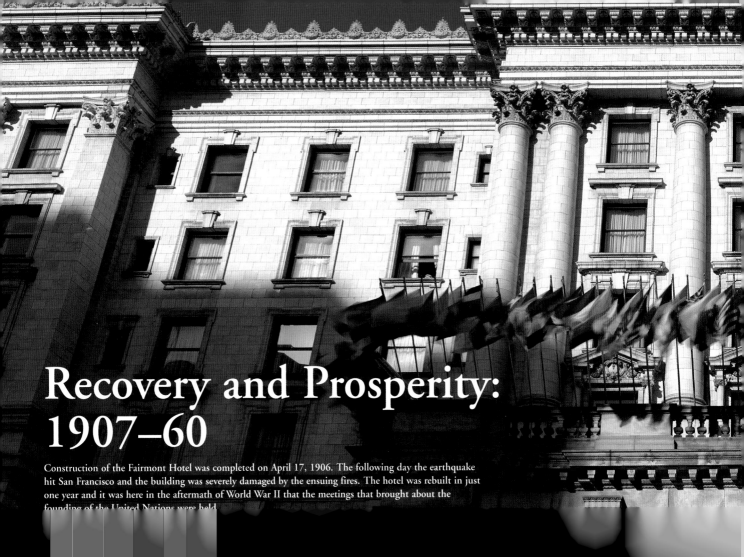

Recovery and Prosperity: 1907–60

Construction of the Fairmont Hotel was completed on April 17, 1906. The following day the earthquake hit San Francisco and the building was severely damaged by the ensuing fires. The hotel was rebuilt in just one year and it was here in the aftermath of World War II that the meetings that brought about the founding of the United Nations were held.

Recovery and Prosperity: 1907–60

Rather than shattering the morale of its citizens the earthquake and fire that had virtually destroyed San Francisco seemed to galvanize the city. The decades that followed saw the construction of many of the most significant and famous landmarks of the modern city. By 1910 the city was almost completely rebuilt and in 1915 it hosted the hugely successful Panama Pacific International Exposition. The previous year had seen the first transcontinental telephone conversation between Alexander Graham Bell in New York and Thomas Watson in San Francisco.

Imposing civic buildings such as the War Memorial Opera House and the Legion of Honor were built in the 1920s and both the Bay Bridge and the Golden Gate Bridge were completed in the mid-1930s. However, the city was also beset by labor troubles during this time, at their nadir two men were shot and killed by police on "Bloody Thursday" (June 5, 1934) during the eighty-three day long West Coast Longshore Strike. The International Longshore and Warehouse Union commemorates the event every year on July 5.

In 1939, the city hosted a second world's fair, the Golden Gate International Exposition, on Treasure Island, next to Yerba Buena Island, in the middle of the Bay Bridge. The Exposition was reopened for a few months in 1940 and following its closure the island became a U.S. Navy base until 1997.

The advent of World War II was to provide an economic boost to San Francisco as the shipyards and other industries began wartime production. In the years following the war San Francisco pursued a controversial program of urban renewal that led to the displacement of many of the African-Americans who had arrived in the Fillmore area to fill the jobs that were created by the war effort.

LEFT: Situated at the corner of Kearny Street and Columbus Avenue, the copper-clad Sentinel Building has been home to Francis Ford Coppola's American Zoetrope Studios since 1972. Work was completed on the building in 1907 following earthquake damage sustained during its construction.

LEFT: Prior to being bought by the Bank of Canton during the 1960s, this building, constructed in 1909, housed the Chinese Telephone Exchange.

ABOVE: A postcard showing the interior of the Chinese Telephone Exchange. The operators at the exchange spoke five Chinese dialects as well as English. The exchange was operational until 1949 when the service became automated.

LEFT: Designed by the architect George Applegarth, the imposing Spreckels Mansion at 2080 Washington Street was built in 1912 for Alma de Bretteville Spreckels, the renowned San Francisco socialite and philanthropist who was the model for the Victory statue in Union Square.

BELOW: The twin spires of Saint Ignatius Church rise above the surrounding buildings. The church is at the heart of the campus of the University of San Francisco. Construction completed in 1914 and it continues to serve as the university's chapel to this day.

LEFT: The architect John Galen Howard designed the Civic Auditorium, which opened in 1915. It still serves as one of San Francisco's foremost concert venues and is also used as a conference center. In 1992 it was renamed the Bill Graham Civic Auditorium in honor of the legendary San Francisco rock promoter who died the previous year.

RIGHT: San Francisco's majestic City Hall was designed by Arthur Brown, whose inspiration for the ornate dome was the St. Peter's Church in Rome. Construction of the building was completed in 1915, just prior to the opening of the Panama Pacific International Exposition of that year. The recently renovated building also houses the Museum of the City of San Francisco.

Panama Pacific International Exposition

Running from February 20th until December 4th, 1915 the Panama Pacific International Exposition was officially held to commemorate the opening of the Panama Canal. However, many people saw it as a chance for San Franciscans to celebrate their city's recovery. Competition to host the Exposition had been fierce, with New Orleans being one of San Francisco's prime rivals, but in 1911 President Taft finally announced that the city had been chosen to host the event.

Although the Exposition was originally planned to be held in Golden Gate Park, the site was eventually switched to reclaimed

marshland in what is now the Marine District. The majority of the magnificent buildings that were assembled for the PPIE were not designed to last any longer than the event itself and were constructed of a mixture of plaster and burlap fiber. Indeed, the bulk of them were taken down after the Exposition and the only one that still stands today is Bernard Maybeck's Palace of Fine Arts. The fair was considered a great success at the time and did an immense amount to restore both civic pride and morale in the city of San Francisco.

A panoramic view of the Panama Pacific International Exposition grounds and buildings under construction in 1914. The frame of the centerpiece Tower of Jewels can be seen in the center of the picture.

ABOVE: A contemporary postcard showing an aerial view of the exposition and the city of San Francisco. The 635-acre site was located between Van Ness Avenue and the Presidio, with its southern border at Chestnut Street and its northern perimeter adjacent to San Francisco Bay.

RIGHT: Fireworks and beams of light illuminate the grounds and buildings of the Panama Pacific International Exposition. The arc of spotlights in the background were shone from a barge known as the "Scintillator" that traversed the bay.

LEFT: The centerpiece of the exposition, The Tower of Jewels, stood 435 feet high and was covered with around 100,000 colored cut-glass "gems" that were lit up at night by over fifty searchlights.

RIGHT: Each of the U.S. states was represented at the exposition with its own building. Seen here is the Ohio Building, which was—with the exception of the dome on the original—an authentic replica of the State House in Columbus.

OHIO

GOV. WILLIS

The Palace of Fine Arts is the only building still standing from the 1915 PPIE. The building was renovated in the 1960s and currently houses the Exploratorium, a science museum that was established by Frank Oppenheimer in 1969.

LEFT: The Hallidie Building at 130 Sutter Street is another San Francisco gem designed by Willis Polk. Completed in 1918, it was the first glass-curtain walled building in the world.

ABOVE: A panoramic view of the
Presidio in 1919. The Palace of the
Fine Arts can be seen in the left of
the picture.

BELOW: A panoramic view of the city,
taken in 1919, overlooking San
Francisco Bay. This photograph
shows the empty fields that only four
years previously had been filled by
the fabulous buildings of the Panama
Pacific International Exposition.

LEFT: Beautiful Victorian mansions line the sides of the famous "crooked" section of Lombard Street, between Hyde and Leavenworth. The eight curved switchbacks were added in the 1920s to enable traffic to climb the hill.

ABOVE: Cars driving down Lombard Street. Vehicular traffic is one way only (downhill) with a speed limit of 10kmh, while pedestrians climb the hill using steps.

119

ABOVE: The magnificent front facade of the Legion of Honor in Lincoln Park. The building of this museum was financed in the 1920s by Alma de Bretteville Spreckels to commemorate Californian servicemen lost in World War I. The building was designed by George Applegarth and based upon the Palais de la Legion d'Honneur in Paris.

RIGHT: The spires of Saints Peter and Paul Church, as seen from Coit Memorial Tower. Also known as the Italian Cathedral and the Fisherman's Church, the building was designed by Charles Fantoni and completed in 1924.

LEFT: Previously the site of a fabulous wooden mansion that was destroyed in 1906, the Mark Hopkins Inter-Continental Hotel was built in 1925. The hotel's most famous feature is the Top of the Mark cocktail lounge on the nineteenth floor, which has spectacular views across the city.

RIGHT: Currently home to the San Francisco Opera, the War Memorial Opera House, along with its twin building the Veterans' Building, was designed by Arthur Brown and built in 1932. It is here that the peace treaty officially ending hostilities between America and Japan was signed in 1951.

LEFT: The 210 foot Coit Tower at the top of Telegraph Hill is one of San Francisco's most recognizable landmarks. Built in 1933 with money bequeathed to the city by Lillie Hitchcock Coit, the tower lobby is decorated with a series of colorful murals commissioned during the Depression to provide work for local artists. From the top of the tower one can enjoy breathtaking views of the North Bay Area.

ABOVE: The Presidio Officers' Club was renovated in the 1930s to give it a Spanish Colonial Revival style look, but the structure still contains sections of the adobe walls of the original Spanish presidio.

Although not as famous as the Golden Gate Bridge, the San Francisco-Oakland Bay Bridge was nonetheless a marvellous feat of engineering. Finished in 1936, one year before the Golden Gate Bridge, the completion of Bay Bridge signaled the end of the line for ferry services across the bay.

Golden Gate Bridge

Prior to the construction of the Golden Gate Bridge the crossing of the Golden Gate Strait was by ferry that ran between the Hyde Street Pier, at the end of Van Ness Avenue, and Sausalito. In the early 1920s the engineer Joseph Straus became convinced that a bridge could and should be built across the strait. Strauss faced stiff opposition to his plans from numerous parties, but eventually his dogged persistence paid off and following the raising of a $35 million bond issue, work finally began on the bridge on January 5, 1933.

Although Strauss is widely accredited as the creator of the bridge he was greatly assisted in its final design by the engineer Charles Ellis and bridge designer Leon Moisseiff. The architect Irving Morrow was responsible for the orange vermillion (also called International Orange) color of the bridge as well as the Art Deco features that decorate it.

On May 27, 1937 the Golden Gate Bridge was opened to pedestrians, witnessed by a crowd of almost 18,000 people. The following day at 09.30am the first cars crossed the bridge. At the time the toll was fifty cents one way and a dollar for the round trip.

RIGHT: The Golden Gate Bridge, as seen from the San Francisco side, with Fort Point in the bottom left. The total length of the bridge, including approaches, is 1.7 miles and each year it is crossed by more than forty million vehicles.

LEFT: Workmen build a catwalk to connect the towers at both sides of the strait so that they could attach the cables for the bridge. Despite the dangers of working at such heights, only twelve men died during the construction of the bridge. This was a phenomenally low figure for such a project at that time and was largely due to innovations that Strauss introduced, such as the mandatory wearing of hard hats and the setting up of a safety net beneath the bridge during construction (the safety net alone is thought to have saved as many as nineteen lives).

RIGHT: The two pylons of the bridge during their construction (the south pylon in the foreground). The hollow pylons stand 746 feet above the water.

LEFT: A view from the top of the South Tower, the two huge cables that span the bridge are 1.4 miles long and three feet wide and are made up of over 80,000 miles (128,747km) of steel wire.

LEFT: The bridge looks particularly enchanting when lit up at night, as seen here, illuminated by over 150 lights of varying strengths.

BELOW: On May 28, 1987, the Golden Gate Bridge celebrated its fiftieth anniversary. It was closed to vehicles for the day and it is estimated that over 300,000 people crowded onto the bridge during the celebrations.

Modern San Francisco: 1961–Today

A sunset view of the brightly lit San Francisco skyline from across the bay. The San Francisco-Oakland Bay Bridge can be seen on the left.

Modern San Francisco: 1961–Today

Modern San Francisco is an eclectic mixture of old and new. Although there is little bar the Mission Dolores that harks back to its Colonial past there are still many homes and buildings from the affluent days of late nineteenth century expansion alongside more recent skyscrapers and high-rises. During the last half of the twentieth century San Francisco frequently made headlines around the world. The 1960s saw the city at the heart of the hippie movement while the kidnapping of heiress Patty Hearst by the Symbionese Liberation Army and the rise of the vocal gay movement in San Francisco marked the 1970s. During the explosion in home computing in the 1980s, with the close proximity of Silicon Valley, the city became synonymous with the rise of this new technology.

The 1980s also saw a resistance to the "Manhattanization" of the city, in both the Financial District and more residential areas, this led to restrictions being placed on the height of new skyscrapers and tower blocks, though in more recent times the pressure to provide housing has led to a relaxation of these constraints. The 1990s saw the boom and bust of the short-lived dot-com era and the election of the first African-American Mayor of San Francisco, Willie Brown. Although, like most major cities around the world, San Francisco struggles with ongoing issues such as the large number of homeless people, the city undoubtedly still retains its unique charm and vibrant atmosphere and is as busy and successful now as at any point in its history.

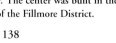

RIGHT: The seventy-five-foot five-tiered pagoda, seen here, is situated in the Peace Plaza of the Nihonmachi Mall in the Japan Center. The center was built in the 1960s as part of a renovation of the Fillmore District.

LEFT: A bird's eye view of Grace Cathedral at 1100 California Street. The cathedral was designed by Lewis P. Hobart and construction was completed in 1964.

ABOVE: The magnificent interior of Grace Cathedral, featuring soaring, arched columns and beautiful art-glass windows designed by Charles Connick.

LEFT: A psychedelic bus crossing an intersection in the Haight-Ashbury district. During the "Summer of Love" in 1967, San Francisco, and the Haight-Ashbury district in particular, was a focal point of the emerging hippie scene.

RIGHT: The fifty-two-storey Bank of America building at 555 California Street is the fifth tallest building on the West Coast and was tallest in San Francisco until the Transamerica Pyramid was built in 1972. The building was designed by Skidmore, Owings & Merrill and Wurster, Bernardi & Emmons and was completed in 1969.

LEFT: Seen here is the gate at the southern entrance of San Francisco's Chinatown. The gate was built in 1970 and bears the inscription "All under heaven is for the good of the people."

RIGHT: An aerial view of St. Mary's Cathedral on Gough Street. The 200 foot building was designed by Pier Luigi Nervi and Pietro Belluschi and built in 1971.

RIGHT: Sitting atop Mount Sutro in west San Francisco like an invading alien from *The War of the Worlds,* The Sutro Tower (lit by red lights, on the right) is a 977 foot antenna tower that is used by television and radio stations to broadcast their signals. Built in 1972, the tower is the only San Francisco structure that can be seen above the fog when it envelops the city.

LEFT: The Transamerica Pyramid, on the right of the picture, is the tallest building in San Francisco. Designed by William Pereira and Associates the building is 853 feet tall and originally housed the headquarters of the Transamerica Insurance and Investment Group. Although this is no longer the case, the pyramid is still used as the company's logo.

ABOVE: Built in 1977, this building on Stockton Street houses the Chinatown Post Office and, on the fourth floor, the historic Kong Chow Temple. The temple was founded in the 1850s and still houses the original nineteenth century altar and statue of Kuan Ti.

A crowd enjoying the antics of the
sea lions at Pier 39. In 1978 the area
was revamped and is now a popular
tourist destination featuring street
performers, restaurants, shops, and
funfair rides.

The Moscone Center, seen here in 1984 when it hosted the Democratic National Convention, is named after the former mayor of San Francisco who was assassinated in 1978. Built in 1981, it is the largest convention center in the city and was part of a scheme to regenerate Yerba Buena Gardens in the Financial District.

RIGHT: The skylight and atrium of the Crocker Galleria in the heart of the Financial District. Built in 1982, this light and spacious high-end shopping area was designed by Skidmore, Owings & Merrill and houses over fifty designer boutiques and multi-cultural restaurants.

The San Francisco Museum of Modern Art was founded in 1935 and moved to its current location, seen here, in 1995. The highlight of this ultra-modern building is the oval skylight that funnels light into the first floor entrance hall.

Designed by Ricardo Legorreta , the UCSF Mission Bay Community Center was opened in October 2005. The four-storey building sits is filled with works of art.

LEFT AND ABOVE: An exterior and an interior view of AT&T Park in the China Basin area on the outskirts of downtown San Francisco. The ballpark has been the home of the San Francisco Giants baseball team since 2000 when it replaced Candlestick Park. It holds 41,503 and was built at a cost of $255 million.

An aerial view of modern San Francisco with a bank of morning fog rolling in from the bay.

Picture Credits

Map on page 9 courtesy of Mark Franklin
Photographs supplied by the Prints and Photographs division of the Library of Congress unless otherwise specified.
Corbis images: Page 2 Richard Cummins; 4-5 Bob Rowan; Progressive Image; 6-7 Richard Berenholtz; 11; 12 Bettmann; 14-15, 74-75, 98-99, 128-129, 135, 136-137, 158-159 Joseph Sohm, Visions of America; 19 Robert Holmes; 20 Mark E. Gibson; 22-23 Darryl Bush/San Francisco Chronicle; 29 Robert Holmes; 30-31 Morton Beebe; 32-33 Michael Freeman; 35 Robert Holmes; 40 Robert Holmes; 46 Bettmann; 47 William Manning; 48-49 Roger Ressmeyer; 53 Robert Holmes; 55 Morton Beebe; 57-58 Lowell Georgia; 58-59 Gerald French; 60 MedioImages; 61; 62 Jan Butchofsky-Houser; 63 Art on File; 68-69 Bettmann; 71 Morton Beebe; 72 Kevin Fleming; 73 Philip Gould; 78 Robert Holmes; 79 Robert Holmes; 80; 81 Kim Kulish; 83; 84 Carl & Ann Purcell; 85 Robert Holmes; 101 Robert Holmes; 102 Carl & Ann Purcell; 103 Rykoff Collection; 105 Philip James Corwin; 107 David Sailors; 110 Lake County Museum; 111 Schenectady Museum; Hall of Electrical History Foundation; 112 Lake County Museum; 112-113 Rykoff Collection; 114-115 Michael T. Sedam; 118 Ron Watts; 119 Goodshoot; 120 Dave G. Houser; 121 Karen Huntt; 122 Morton Beebe; 124 Catherine Karnow; 126-127 Chuck Keeler, Jr.; 130 Bettmann; 131 Underwood & Underwood; 132-133 Gerald French; 134 ML Sinibaldi; 138-139 Robert Holmes; 140 Robert Holmes; 141 Robert Holmes; 142-143 Henry Diltz; 143 Morton Beebe; 144 ImageShop; 145 Charles E. Rotkin; 146-147 Roger Ressmeyer; 148 Goodshoot; 149 Phil Schermeister; 150-151 Gerald French; 152 Bettmann; 153 Morton Beebe; 154 Craig Lovell; 155 Art on File; 156-157 BSF/NewSport; 157 Reuters